75 and Fabulous: Reflections

S H E R R I M O R R

Fulton Books, Inc.
Meadville, PA

Published by Fulton Books 2021

ISBN 978-1-63860-147-0 (paperback)
ISBN 978-1-63860-148-7 (digital)

Printed in the United States of America

Sherri and I met on a walk to discuss her joining ChaiVillageLA, a virtual village for active older adults who want to age in place by creating a nurturing community that is keeping its 250 members independent and yet connected through supportive services and a rich variety of programs. It was a successful walk: Sherri joined the village and is now an active board member emphasizing her commitment to volunteerism.

Her book, written during the pandemic, is full of family stories often explaining why and how she functioned (or didn't) in this period of social isolation. Reading those stories makes you feel like you are on a walk with a friend you can trust who can help you get good at getting older.

Rabbi Laura Geller, Rabbi Emerita of Temple Emanuel of Beverly Hills, cofounder of ChaiVllageLA, and co-author with her late husband Richard Siegel of Getting Good at Getting Older.

Laura Geller
Rabbi Emerita
Temple Emanuel of Beverly Hills
310-927-1239 (Cell)
www.rabbilaurageller.com
Co-founder, ChaiVillageLA.org
Chair, Synagogue Village Network
Co-author, *Getting Good at Getting Older*
(Behrman House, 2019

Sherri is a "people's person" and that is reflected in her anecdotal way of storytelling. Her co-worker with his whistling, the poor fundraiser (a word her grandpa Louie wouldn't know if you tortured him) climbing up the stairs and all other folks in her *stettel*—rebranded by Sherri as her Kibbutz—I could relate to each and every one of them.

The Jewish, professional and family lives of Sherri are all intertwined and portrait the funny, serious, dedicated, loving, disliking, agonizing person I learned to love and appreciate over the years of our mutual professional and personal development. Read the book and you will know why.

Yariv M. Sultan
Founder GlobalCan: Strategic Solutions for Nonprofits
Globalcan.co.il
Israel

Sherri is funny, honest, deep, and insightful. Her writing is inspiring. I cried, I laughed and kept nodding my head in agreement, knowing precisely what she was talking about, grateful for her eloquent articulation. Everyone should take the time to read these beautiful stories regardless of their age because they are beautifully written and create a cathartic experience that eases the quarantine trauma we all have experienced.

Naomi Ackerman
Founder, Executive Director
The *Advot* Project http://www.theadvotproject.org/

"The only thing you have, is what you give away."

Marcia Burnam 1928-2020

Wise, funny, and true, Sherri Morr's open-hearted debut collection reminds us that what really matters is love, family, and a decent beach chair.

Kathy Ebel, *Claudia Silver to the Rescue*

GRATITUDE

Appreciated the most are my sons, my husband, and the scores of generous people I have met throughout my journey as a fundraiser on behalf of noble and worthy causes.

Sherri Morr

Contents

PROLOGUE

These thoughts and experiences of COVID-19 are based on my life experiences. This is not my life story; on the other hand, there is much of me in it. Some days I wake up and am not sure what day it is. The days, you see, all seem the same. Thank goodness for *The New York Times.* If it's Monday, it's Sports; Tuesday: Science; Wednesday: Food; and so on. At my age, it's common to have this little brief confusion; fortunately, I can rely on the paper to steer me. Looking back as we approach 2021, I shall recall many things; uppermost it's the sameness of each day and how much courage it takes to read the paper, see the numbers, read about deaths and more dying, and read about lack of hospital beds, decreasing oxygen, not enough ventilators, which state is allowing evictions and not, and the worst, the absolute worst, no leadership in our country. With twenty-something days left in this administration who breeds chaos, I am hopeful, even feel teary-eyed relief, that our situation will get better.

When the pandemic hit and caused me to stay home, my young adult sons, that are three thousand miles away, watched me like a hawk. The first incident of disapproval was going to Macy's for the Jockey underwear sale. "No, I cannot buy online," I defended myself. No, I did not wear a mask. I quickly breezed in and then out. Besides this was pre-masks. Pre-March 16 when my school where I worked closed down, and I was jobless.

Before that, our handsome governor used to be known as the handsome mayor, who bravely legalized gay marriage in 2004 in San Francisco, declared people in love should be able to marry regardless of their gender. Ah yes, he is handsome and thought to flatten the COVID-19 curve just by staying home—a real "we can do it" attitude. Gavin Newsom (some name, right?) became an icon to my young adult sons who tried to enforce their own iconic rules for staying safe. "You are compromised," they said. There is smoking. Your lungs are probably shot. Pneumonia, kidney disease, and cancer are your pandemic mantra words. They alone should keep you home.

What I did not realize as I began the isolation on March 16 was that I had much trauma experience, and the absence of being busy would lead me to think about the past. Think way too much. At home alone (initially), being with my own thoughts, I could not help from connecting to other traumas in my life. I did not have to go to work. I did not have to run unimportant errands like picking up the dry cleaning. I no longer had numerous phone calls to make, and I did not concern myself with what to wear because I was not going anywhere! I liked staying home.

People have one trauma, they begat another. Oh, I am not speaking of the regular stuff like divorce, infertility, dependence versus independence feelings, and taking care of oneself versus someone else, or "you said you would take care of me," but having good jobs but continually wanting better jobs, the hole in my heart, and the empty years of a father who abandoned his family, to become I am not sure what, but to shed his responsibility to family, parents, and children.

This was an unanticipated aspect of the pandemic; perhaps it's a tarnished lining of the stay-at-home rules. I knew even at the young age of seven what it was like to have the rug pulled—pulled in such a way life cannot return to what it was. The hole is so deep, so vacant, and at such a young age. There was no complete recovery. So, in my social isolation, I thought about those years and their pain and how they formed me and how they unconsciously made me a different person—one who begged to please. Just a few words could reverse a sunny day to darkness. How I did not understand and how scary it was. In a movie version, someone would take the children aside and sensitively explain the situation. These were my childhood years and not a movie.

1

Every Moment Every Day

I used to live in Sherman Oaks, California. Even though I've been gone for several decades, I still maintain certain contacts and services in the San Fernando Valley in Los Angeles. Yesterday was one of those days I decided to visit the area. I used my extra time to meander on Ventura Boulevard in the Studio City area. I felt a level of sad nostalgia seeing so many of my old haunts shuttered and closed, empty, and dark. The few stores open had metal gates to choose who they let in. After seeing the homeless on the streets, lying on bus benches, too infirm to rise up even, it's understandable to have to protect their businesses and staff especially during COVID-19.

The lack of continued federal relief has more than increased people on the street. They have no resources for housing. They lost everything in a flash—no warning really, no savings perhaps ever, and barely living paycheck to paycheck, and that's so common for the most integral service workers. Now city officials say there are close to seventy thousand people living on the streets in the greater Los Angeles area. This count does not include people sleeping in cars.

Prior to the pandemic, many like myself rarely thought about this aspect of the population. They cleaned our houses, served our food in restaurants, and worked at seasonal sites or as handymen, gardeners, and small job people. They were paid. They received tips and a holiday bonus. Now look where they are.

I was shocked to see the condition of these homeless people: shoeless, filthy feet, totally dirty besides wearing rags—things one reads about in books or sees in B-level movies. This is real, both frustrating and anger producing. In Los Angeles, I complain plenty about the homeless in my area. Our streets are cockroach-ridden. Many people are begging, leaning against buildings, some with pets plus bags of belongings. The trash and the smell are overwhelming. When I contacted my local city representative's office after many unreturned phone calls (I do not give up easily), I reached someone who told me the businesses are responsible for the sidewalks, not the city or county. They only are responsible for the streets where cars, trucks, and buses traverse. When I think about what people spend in these stores and shops and can pay up to $9 for a Shabbat challah (and that does not include the cakes and special cookies), the situation begs me to say, to shout aloud, and to almost cry. Is this America?

Last week I was waiting in the parking lot at a drugstore. It was a typical Los Angeles winter-hot day, and the shoeless man leaning on the wall was crying about needing new socks. I walked over and gave him $5. Then he said, "Please go inside and buy me a pair of socks. My feet are blistering from these shoes that do not fit. They won't let me in without shoes." He wanted to return the $5 to me so I could pay for his socks. I did not do it.

I said, "No, just go in yourself. Put your shoes on, and go in." Then I had to leave. Sad story, right? It's easy to give money if you can, but getting involved is not so easy at all.

This is COVID-19. This is the pandemic. In Los Angeles, we are close to running out of beds for sick people. Some, maybe many more will die. We are in the second major lockdown. I was only out of the house to pick up someone in that parking lot. Someone I knew. I had given the homeless man money before he started screaming about needing socks.

A few years ago, I used to make sandwiches and give them to homeless people in my neighborhood. Later on, I walked by and saw the sandwiches that were left—half unwrapped and half eaten in the street. I guessed they did not like my sandwiches. We, all of us, who can and who have housing, food, and security at any level, must be grateful every day, every moment. This could be the silver lining of our personal COVID-19 experience.

2

Do I Have It?

So many issues. I cannot see without my glasses. I cannot hear even with hearing aids. I cannot walk more than twenty-five minutes without my lower back pain killing me. After driving two hours, my right leg is aching. I cannot eat three meals a day like normal people, and actually I think those people are weird. I cannot speak even to my best friends for more than twenty minutes on the phone without feeling they are plain boring. I cannot say a nice word to my husband without some form of criticism built in. I cannot make myself check in with my sister. I am just plain cranky especially when the conversation may infer some slight hint of critical content. I do not care that everyone is going through this now. I am not everyone.

I cannot breathe with my mask on. My nose runs, and my eyes water. I have become a walking box of tissues, found crumpled everywhere I step or worse in my jacket pockets (and I have a lot of jackets). In March, when we went into lockdown, I went through every pocket, and after finding way too many to count, I discarded them in a plastic bag in the outside garbage. I washed my hands repeatedly and then sanitized them repeatedly. My mother was the same way—Kleenex in every pocket. It must be true that we women become our mothers. *OY!* (Yiddish for "my goodness.")

My hands feel like the severe side of a nail file. My hearing is worse than normally bad even with new expensive, high-powered hearing aids. I lose about one earring a week in the process of removing my mask. I refuse to give up earrings. Never. I prefer to lose one and keep the single earrings lonely and alone in a lovely sentimental box (among my small box collection). On the other hand, I wonder if the masks can hide bad breath, or spitting as you speak, or missing teeth? Especially on the days when I am too down to even brush my teeth or take my daily meds. I have tried cannabis gummies mainly because I love candy—especially candy that sticks to your teeth, in spite of thousands of dollars of dental work throughout my life. So far, no respite from my issues and fearful to keep taking more. I do have limits once in a while.

In normal times (okay most of the time), I am a giving, fun person who has a unique sense of humor. I usually have amazing and unusual ideas for which I am lauded. Now I could care less about anything unusual. Trips, projects or sights, forget about all that. It just takes too much energy. Did I mention I have no energy?

I do like to talk about where I might be going. Invariably I go nowhere. The only thing that makes me smile and tear up over with pride and happiness is watching videos and FT with my almost-two-year-old granddaughter who lives with her parents three thousand miles away. In October, numbers were down in New York, so I snuck in for a quick five-day visit. It was worth the risk. Totally worth it—being tested three times, sitting alone on a five-hour flight, masked, and out of available alcohol (did I mention cocktail hour is at 4:00 p.m.? Okay, maybe 3:00 p.m.). With no one to talk to, I could make up a crazy story of who I am. Decades ago, I told a seatmate I was a rabbi. Poor guy could not get over how someone like me was a rabbi. This was way before the idea that women could even be a rabbi, nor even look like one (whatever that means). He told me he thought all rabbis wore black hats and had long beards. Well, I told him, "I am a different kind of rabbi."

What is going to become of me, I wonder. I am so fearful of COVID-19. I worry I may just get it because I think about it too much. If I do get it, I prefer to die. I have this stupid thought that I will have time to swallow a handful of meds and avoid the horrific descriptions of how these poor folks have died. I do worry I may not remember to take them or even know where they are kept.

When I had my flu shot, the reaction felt severe. My body felt as though it had been hit by a truck or a steamroller. Every part hurts. My chest was heavy, and my legs ached. I was moaning out loud all night in bed, tossing and turning, groaning at every movement. Then a revisit to the "do I want to die issue?" Maybe yes, but quickly, please. Do I have it? Is this it?

3

It's All about My Hair

My hair is out of control. My whole life is out of control. One moment I am fantasizing about a trip to New York in July to see our eighteen-month-old granddaughter (whom I have not seen in six months), and the next moment I am too depressed to do much other than decide which cake to buy and then eat. In one sitting! Oy! It has been more than three months since I've had a haircut, and color has graced my head of hair. It is five inches longer and now the awfully drab color of mousey brown from during the Berkeley Free Speech Movement in 1965.

I had graduated to scrunchies and plastic rubber bands that pinch and had cut the bangs myself. On three separate occasions, I called my person periodically to ask if they are considering when they might reopen. She does respond kindly I might add but with no information of any real value.

Mid last week, I drove by a small salon like a ten-minute walk from my house and saw lights on and people inside. Damn, I missed the opportunity to swerve around and stop in. This quiet neighborhood salon is where two adorable sisters do nails all day long—manis, pedis, fills, acrylic, gel, whatever you need to have long-looking, well-kept fingers in a quiet, orderly, and very clean environment. If you point a lot in your work using your fingers, you feel my pain. If you use your hands while speaking, you also understand my professional oriented needs.

After more than three months, my nails look sort of chalky as though they have been exposed to a disease—short and well filed but just plain unattractive.

Yes, you are correct. I have called the sisters as well, but they are waiting for verbal permission from the mayor. Gee, is there no one who can make an independent decision?

I have always had fine, textured hair and very little weight or body. My sister, four years older and quite attractive, had beautiful curly, wavy hair. Hair to be envied certainly. My mom and our relatives known as the "aunts" applied Toni permanents to my hair, and the result, other than gagging from the toxic smell, was frizz—plain, dry-looking frizz, no more body than before, and still mousey brown. Finally, my relatives gave up. Even my grandma would say, "Oy, my Sherrilah. You poor thing. You have hair just like mine." A true shame. So, growing up, my hair was a burden. To keep me happy, we would cut off the frizz and keep it long enough to be a nice, neat ponytail.

As a teenager, I combed peroxide through and sat in the sun to treat the mousy brown into a kind of dirty brown look—a tremendous improvement. COVID-19 has given a green shine to my hair. The blond, the brown, and the hidden gray has caused this sheen. My hair has been colored since 1967 when I went frosted blond. I have not seen my original color since that time (not that I have any desire to). Because of the dye, my hair has actually become a bit thicker. It could be trained, set, heat rolled, or blown dry into a terrific look. Better than my younger years for sure.

As part of social isolation, no haircuts are allowed. Oh, some friends have stylists come to their home to apply the necessities of life which is looking good, and hair plays a pretty specific role. You enter with nice makeup, swinging healthy hair, and put together stylishly. You're set to go. But then, I am not going anywhere nor seeing anyone during COVID-19. I wear the same clothes almost daily. Why get dressed? For what or for whom? When you work at home, be comfy. Wear your sweats or pajamas. All virtual calls are only from the waist up. Pretty easy, right? On Zoom calls, my hair looks pretty good, not sure how or why, but it does. Is this a silver lining? Maybe just stay on Zoom and practice my whole life virtually. A different type of recluse, perhaps?

Sherri & Arlene

4

Beyond Sweats

A day in the life at home since March 2020.

Just read in the news that women (okay—and some men) in the United Kingdom may have stopped carrying bags during the pandemic. This lack of carrying, the article said, may indicate a future with no purses, backpacks, expensive and fancy name brand bags, and no jewel-studded small clutch bags. Do we care? It's what I refer to as beyond fluff. Is this possible? What do they do with their stuff? Is this a rumor begun by Queen Elizabeth, knowing those carry bags she uses must be empty? I mean she needs no wallet, no ID, no cash, or credit cards. Lipstick maybe? A tissue, a hankie? No little notebook to write down something of value. People, she has people, real live humans who do this work for her. Probably one of the attendants must have a clean mask ready at any time. Unless members of the Royal cousin's club rotate this effort pro bono. The crown must show some frugality after all.

I do not recall an affinity to bags. My first recollection was when my mom gave me a generous check to buy a new bed quilt which she pronounced "well past its prime." This was in the 1970s. Walking through the store, I passed the bag section and was immediately in awe over how beautiful they were. I have no recollection (even then when I was young) of ever looking at bags, let alone looking longingly at bags—the softness, the colors, and in so many styles. I could not help myself. I did not agonize. I was in love, thus merely picked out one I liked and returned home with no new quilt but with a hip, classy, very soft leather backpack.

Who even noticed except my mother and that was only because she was visiting.

Having been a remote worker for the last ten years, what to wear at home was never an issue or a thought even. I just did what I felt. But, now, of course with COVID-19, thousands of people are pivoted to home offices, sharing space, time, and attention with whole families who have also been driven home to work. I would have doubted what to wear at home would have become a national issue, but boy was I wrong. Discussions, articles, Zoom calls and more have all been discussed from sweats to bras to bathrobes to shorts / T-shirts, and to pajamas. So, talking about what sort of purse to carry on the rare moments of leaving your space seems odd. But it garnered a crowd especially for women; fashion shoots actually have continued, so what do I know? I will admit to the fact that emerging from the house on rare occasions demands a number of supplies. A big purse/carryall because the pandemic requires mask, extra mask, hand sanitizer, hand cream, gloves, snack/water, Kleenex, wallet, phone, ID, notebook/pens, and extra glasses. Other than bottles, diapers, and a change of clothes, it reminds me of getting out of the house with a new baby.

Most days I wake up when I do. Occasionally there is an early call, then I have to trust an alarm rather than myself.

I have coffee. I take my meds. I browse the papers we receive daily and skim through my phone. Then I check to see what is scheduled. I decide to shower or not, fresh clothes or a repeat of yesterday, and a few morning rituals. At my computer by ten or ten thirty, and this is after/during yogurt parfait. Morning calls are a must before some businesses shut for lunch or send calls to a message center where callbacks can be days of phone tag. And this only speaks to calls on PST. Reaching a human is tough these days with all the staff decreases. Texting does not work for describing a personal or private work issue.

Three hours of solid work: writing, producing professional documents for clients, Zoom calls, calling people I know who are not "taking lunch," reading professional articles, revising to-do lists, researching on people, organizing, volunteering work, and updating my calendar.

2:00–3:00 p.m.: lunch break/nap
4:00–5:00 p.m.: more of the above, maybe a walk
6:00 p.m.: dinner with husband, maybe
8:00–10:00 p.m.: answering/clearing emails, more research, or writing
Enough: Go to bed and read

This is a flexible routine. In between any and all of the list above, I may start a soup, compile a grocery list, open the mail, or check in calls to my sister or young adult sons who monitor me like a hawk. I also contact my *chevra* (Hebrew for close friends). The good news during this time is I am primarily accountable to myself; I like this a lot. Using this freedom allows me to think. To consider what we are living through, creating unfortunate history.

When the pandemic began, I read up on other world health crises and thought I had a sense of how bad such a crisis could be. I was not prepared, no matter how much I had read. We have been very lucky in our family—with serious monitoring, we are made more grateful every day, to live every day. But we still worry, fearful, but have the wherewithal to keep informed of the reality of suffering and have courage. There really is no typical day because the news moves pretty quickly and that informs our day, our mood, and our sensitivities. I will read, watch a movie, and take a nap. I wish it were more, less of a bore.

I am my only supervisor, and often I have to self-motivate to accomplish productivity. I do use my time often to send articles of interest to colleagues, friends, or others. This has become self-motivating as I feel so happy to have others enjoy a cartoon or a tongue in cheek but serious essay about wearing masks at a funeral. In the old days, I often mailed them through our trusted post office service. Now during the pandemic, making others smile, nod, reduce depression, or boredom or feeling alone gives me tremendous gratitude. Indeed.

5

75 and Fabulous: My COVID-19 Birthday

Yes, it's true. I am really and truly seventy-five! I have done the math a few times, and so it's confirmed. I have even looked at my yellowing birth certificate. It's shocking to be this age. I never imagined I would live this long. However, now that I am (still) here, I am pretty happy to be alive and relatively well, considering it all.

On a regular birthday (as in not such a big number and as in not during a medical crisis of the entire world), I would be going to lunch with friends, out to dinner with my husband, and any local available children—maybe a museum or theatre or a facial or luxury care service that's just for me. Not this year. Who could do anything luxurious when millions are hungry, jobless, and homeless living on the streets. Or worse, it's all sadder and full of fear and uncertainty, more than I could have ever imagined.

So, we are hunkering down, socially isolating ourselves, participating in numerous Zoom concerts, book talks, cooking, self-help classes, and reading as a real activity opposed to reading to help one fall asleep and block out the pain. I like a quiet birthday with less fussing and all those calls and smiles and saying how happy I am. It's not the end of the world to even have to be alone on your birthday, although I would not admit to being alone. After all, I do my best thinking alone. I arrive at bright, creative ideas when by myself and recall nice memories, good times, and positive thoughts of the past. And on my birthday, I especially think of past birthdays because growing up in my family, birthdays were a big deal.

When I was young, I always had a party filled with all the usual birthday accouterments. I loved the presents, the attention, and the cake. As I grew up, I was not so comfortable with the attention but still to this day even at "seventy-five and fabulous," I love the cake. My family lore for birthdays was pretty simple because I was born on Mother's Day in 1945. My family (the entire clan: grandparents, aunts and uncles, and cousins) always made a very big deal out of Mother's Day, and my birthday was swept along with that.

My birthday any given year could fall on any day of the week, but regardless of that fact, it was always celebrated on Mother's Day. I received my gifts all day, and that was special in one form or another. And ultimately my family went to dinner or a late brunch at a restaurant. All of us could have been as many as twenty people, and that did not include the stray relatives who might have wormed their way into my Grandpa Louie having to pay for even more people. Louie was blunt, on the dictatorial side. When he said we were doing to dinner at 4:00 p.m., it was not open for discussion. When he said we were going to Burroughs restaurant, it was not a choice. When he gave me dirty looks for always ordering the same dinner, I could tear up out of embarrassment. The waitresses, with nameplates on the frilly floral hankies pinned to their uniform, responded to his flirts and smiled

29

at me when I was close to tears for ordering something not expensive. It's as though they implied, "It's okay, honey, men are like that." There was no room for discussion when Louie was in charge.

Every woman received a carnation, which he personally went to buy. Even if you were not a mother, you got a flower because you have a mother or had one before she died. As the birthday girl, I did not get a flower. I had received my presents in the morning. You see it was easy because we all (my grandparents, the four brothers, and their families) lived in the same apartment building. We could gather in any apartment we so desired. And never had to ask for permission. I could just holler out, "I'm going to Aunt Sylvia's" and walk down two flights of stairs. So, on my birthday, I would wander the stairs stopping in to the different apartments to accept my presents. And most assuredly a few cookies along the way. I assumed my parents knew where I was, and they rarely were looking for me or missing me enough to question my whereabouts. Back to Burroughs, my restaurant treat was a cake, always grand (once with sparklers even) and joyous, rowdy singing. Yes, I loved it. When Thursday came, and it was my true birthday, it was not unusual for anyone, not one of them, to say one birthday word!

Now onto the pandemic! I wash my hands probably more than ever and longer. I follow up with a good size douse of hand sanitizer (thank you, Purell) then walk around swishing them in the air so they will dry. I use a keto cream from my ENT doctor inside my nostrils because part of getting older has somehow created dryness inside my nose, resulting in dandruff-like flakes (charming, right?). I have to touch my face to do this. Don't ask. I drink a lot of liquids, and I am a remote worker (since 2010) when I retired. I work from my home office (aka the den), doing contract work. My husband now shares the workspace; who knew he whistled? We each have our own desks, but when we have work-related virtual calls, one of us moves out of the space into the living room or dining room table. We cannot use the smaller table in the kitchen because it's usually covered with the several newspapers we receive daily—not much room for people let alone office accouterments.

We are pretty casual about it—no spreadsheets, no calendars with stars, and several trips back to our desks to remember phones, notepads, coffee cups, pens, and a nail file (in case it's a boring call). You know with no manicurist out and about, it's a perfect time to file my nails. We are old enough to comically suggest, "Next time have your girl call my girl." We eat a lot—not much baking to speak of but quite a few creative soups. Three meals daily are for some regular people. However as an experienced remote worker (and not regular), I have adjusted my eating to twice a day, at 10:00 a.m. and 2:00 p.m. Maybe a few snacks too.

The "seventy-five and fabulous" celebration began one full week before my actual birthday. Calls started coming, emails, and presents. The first day, I received flowers with a balloons, and the second day six (yes, Virginia, there is a Santa) pints of designer flavored ice cream. They came in a huge box with dry ice and two pages of instructions on how to unpack, how to let sit out, and ultimately eat. Plenty of challah loaves had to rearrange themselves to share the freezer with these beautifully and artfully designed cartons with lavish names like Coffee & Milk or Vanilla Brambleberry Crumble. All of this made me happy and perhaps a little less fearful when reading increasing COVID-19 deaths or enjoying hearing that the president had said testing is available everywhere. For everyone, the news descriptions and photos of those subjecting themselves to take care of others were heartbreaking. Yes, I felt pretty annoyed with myself for wondering which ice cream flavor to serve with Shabbat dinner.

My young adult sons who had masterminded this seemingly polish wedding called, and we had many teary calls of thank you and gratitude. They had been overly generous, and I get very emotional thanking them. When I think about how they have expressed our closeness and their appreciation for me as a role model, I worry if I paid enough attention to them, and I tend to become *fahklempt* (Yiddish for "ready to cry") very quickly.

Before I knew it, it was Sunday! Hurrah, Mother's Day! I love being a mom, in spite of my complaining during the hard years like when they came home after six weeks at summer camp, and I was happy to see them and their smelly socks. But two days later, I was begging for school to start. It's hard to be a mom and nice all the time. No one really tells you how demanding and emotional it is, and speaking about it to other moms and dads is just TMI and embarrassing.

Lots of calls and texts in the morning, FB wishes, and even FaceTime with my granddaughter—this sixteen-month-old treasure and gift to our entire family who can say "Happy Birthday, Nana." Oh my.

In the afternoon, it's time for the Zoom "seventy-five and fabulous" call with family including cousins, elderly aunts (OMG, I am elderly too), nephews who created an original take on a Fleetwood Mac's 1977 album *Rumours*, and a quiz to beat any *Jeopardy* questions I have ever heard. Most of my family calls me "SherriBerry," which emanated from my eating berries on a very regular and repeated basis. There were a few renditions of "Sherri, Can You Come Out Tonight?" And then some pretty funny stories including one where my ten-year-old cousin, and I (yes, I was ten once) was stealing cigarettes from my grandma's purse while she was glued to her soaps on TV. We smoked them too.

The last two days before my actual birthday, I went back to being in isolation—walking, eating, reading, thank goodness sitting in the sun, oiling up, and working on my first tan of the summer. The masks cause my nose to run, my eyes to tear up, and my glasses to fog up, and the strings behind my ears have to share their space with my hearing aids. When I remove or adjust the straps, the hearing aids become dislodged and fall out. When I am speaking to someone six feet apart, I can barely hear them because their own speech is muffled, and possibly one of my hearing aids has lost its placement. What a life, right?

On my actual birthday, my sons sent an amazing birthday cake—four thick layers tall, amply filled with assorted berries and buttercream frosting. I ate it all day, then sporadically the next day, and by then I had a bellyache. What to glean from all of this is how lucky that people care; no matter the circumstances, it's *okay* to stop and celebrate. I was happily exhausted when it was over. The memory will stay with me forever. I do not need any more big birthday celebrations, and I hope for never, ever, not another one, ever of COVID-19.

Be sure to wash your hands!

6

Me, My Heating Pad, and COVID-19

In late February, I slipped taking a lovely, relaxing bath. I may have put in too much oil and bath salts. But hurrah, I did not fall, but in the process of saving myself, I heard a loud crack on one side of my lower back. Since I have decreased hearing and wear hearing aids, it had to be loud given I heard it. I was a bit achy, but by the next morning, I could barely walk (this is the short story). I used some heat and limped along in a relatively busy day of meetings. After some meetings, someone had to assist me to my car and carry my briefcase (I do not travel light).

They practically folded me into the driver's seat. Somehow, I made it home, reverting immediately to the heating pad, and called my doctor to get an x-ray. Did I break something? I have not had back or muscle problems except for an almost rotator cuff surgery from lifting a large heavy suitcase (again no traveling light) off the conveyor belt, but as I said, this is the short story.

After the x-ray, the doctor said the results were unremarkable. I do not know why a doctor would use such terminology when a patient is in dire pain and taking Vicodin. It is downright offensive; indeed, I believe I am a remarkable person. Little about me is unremarkable. Even my therapist agrees. Alas, this short story continues. The doctor (as most orthopedics do) instructed me to seek physical therapy. (All orthopedics do this. Do not get me started.)

After two weeks of PT, I felt better and improved and still had almost intimate relations with my heating pad. Then came the coronavirus and along with it the shutdown of the world as we know it. No nothing! Aside from my grooming necessities, no going out for dinner, lunch, or breakfast, no walking with my walking group, no seminars, no in-person meetings, and maybe the worst no movie theaters. No museums, concerts, or live theatre, and beaches are closed. WTF? This is my life. All of the listed are what I spend my time doing. Am I supposed to just stay home and veg out on TV and books? I know, I know. There are worse things, but I am extremely bored and in pain. The final straw was, of course, when PT called and said they were closing…no more PT. Without PT, it took about a week for me to be back in full on pain. Yes, I did the exercises at home but only the easy ones. After two weeks, I remembered a friend had recommended a chiropractor if I ever needed one. Hah. I could not dial fast enough, and in a short time, I had a call back and an appointment for the next day. Someone must be watching over me.

Speaking of watching, I have two young adult sons living on the East Coast. They have good jobs. One has a handsome partner, and the other one has a very attractive wife and an adorable twenty-one-month-old little girl. Under normal circumstances, we are in regular contact and generally have a great relationship. At this time during COVID-19, my sons call me, watch me, and guide me to all my activities. If they call me in the grocery store, I do not answer. If they FT me while having my nails done, surely I do not answer. They will FT me to be sure I am not in a crowd of people. They insisted I cancel the housekeeper lest I pick up something from her. All of their questions are open-ended, rather than do not do that. They speak to me the way I raised them, "Gee, Mom, are you sure that's a good idea?" Am I cleaning and then disposing of any delivered food-related items like plates or utensils? Upon telling them I was seeing a doctor and going to this office, they strongly asked if I thought that was wise. When I pleaded, I needed pain relief and it was hard to walk, they were silent. They, for years as I have gotten older, would like to keep me in a bubble. Remarkable.

The chiropractor actually helped me. He did some PT and a few jolts, and the pain was less. But after a full week of back jolting, the pain began to return. Back to a different orthopedist and an MRI showing remarkable problems of the disc impinging on nerves. Ah, so that's why there is so much pain. Remarkable.

So now there is a plan—more PT and if no consistent improvement, an epidural with cortisone but no surgery. Hurrah. With this combination and meds, I should improve. Meaning I may return to being a nicer person, more patient, less cranky, might even be able to move or sit without my ever-present heating pad, and might even bake something. Remarkable.

Follow the Money

I grew up living communally, like on a kibbutz. Not that I knew what a kibbutz was at the time. Our extended family lived in one apartment building—three brothers, their wives, and a total of seven children among them plus, my grandparents and a younger son. Sixteen in total. They fled from Brooklyn in the early 1950s to Virginia to start a business of "Mama Papa" grocery stores. They did this, simply put, to make money and make something of their lives—all together as a family.

Money was all important to them. My grandfather was a bit of a dictator, and perhaps we all lived in the same building to be sure the brothers (aka the boys) followed his plan—included, but perhaps not planned, was tremendous competition. When Grandpa Louie decided to buy another grocery store, it was to make more money and, of course, alleviate any competition. Any group dinner and any holiday gatherings included speaking of money.

How much they had, which store was making the most money, and if any of the clan was spending money needlessly. I recall one event where one of my aunts had purchased a plastic floral arrangement for her table. (They were quite popular then.) Grandpa Louie basically cross-examined her about cost (which he was appalled after hearing), why she needed it, and did they even have a place to put such a thing. He may have even asked, by looking around the room, if anyone else had such an item. Her husband sat silently through this diatribe and the other sisters-in-law as well. Although it was killing me not to say how pretty it was, my cousins and I just looked at our feet. We all had seen it. Living one floor up or one floor down, we roamed quite freely. We had agreed we had never seen anything like it. Such fat, colorful, and juicy-looking fruit we could not eat.

Everything had a money connotation. Years later when my cousins were older and some of the girls were getting engaged, my grandma would ask two questions: How big is the ring, and what does the boy do for a living?—money, once again.

Some say I am in the money business because of those growing up years. I have worked in raising money for the last four decades. It's not the same as making money, but it is money after all. And I do always think, as part of my work, a lot about money. Who has it? Are they charitable? Are they interested in society or feel responsible toward those less fortunate? I recall from my childhood a man coming to our house to ask for money for Israel and my father putting money in an envelope. I doubt this man, having to walk up two more flights of stairs, asked Grandpa Louie.

Two thousand and twenty will be remembered for many things. With millions of people suddenly and unexpectedly unemployed, there was a huge lack of money with little warning. All of this very serious, life challenging, and life threatening. COVID-19 and the politics of social action and human rights are not a great mix. One could be worried about dying from COVID-19, being attacked on the streets in violent protests, or seeing totally misunderstood scenarios result in single individual shootings. It's just not a safe time for citizens in America. And it's not a secure time either. Our society has mechanisms that respond to hardships in people's lives. In 2020, these mechanisms have not been applied quickly. The very individuals (both men and women) elected to represent us have been more interested in hearing themselves speak than urgently acting on providing the very basic needs of people in distress. The message of 2020 might be not to count on your country. The mechanisms of our country often considered "charity" have always provided for a system to step in as a means of addressing public needs. Having all this time on our hands, we cannot help but wonder what is the delay. It's not a new concept. In spite of this, or maybe because of these situations, raising money continued. In fact, the "ask" came from hundreds, perhaps thousands of individual institutions. I would suggest it's fair to say since COVID-19 began, *everyone* was asking.

For the sake of history, consider Andrew Carnegie's 1889 Gospel of Wealth. His foundation and those of other captains of industry were able to affect the common good and had far-reaching effects on education, culture, science, and public health. These individual millionaires stepped up and gave away their excess money to help others. In a sense, individual giving was born. It has grown to be an industry—a business of supporting people, institutions, hospitals, mental health centers, low-income housing, and services for at-risk elderly, just to mention a few. Giving has graduated to be considered philanthropy, development, fundraising, or advancement. Sophisticated names that see a need and find the means to address it.

Money is no longer a taboo topic. Give now while you can target your interests. Give for later after you are gone but dictated before you died how you expect your resources to be divided among your variety of priorities. Give on Monday or Tuesday. Give smaller donations because theoretically many can give $5 or $10, and they can be as meaningful as larger ones. Accumulated small donations became sought after as never before. When the internet became a lifestyle, giving online became like a wide-open horse race.

Evidence of this was after 9/11 when the population, so devastated by the worst terror attack in America's history, realized they could make a donation *and* still go out to dinner or to a movie. Accumulated small giving increased during this time. Before, these smaller gifts were a result of phone solicitations and something called direct mail—envelopes filled with up to five documents sent to purchased lists.

The pandemic has unleashed a veritable flood of being asked to give money. The pandemic has also birthed new organizations. With all the new organizations and urgent institutional needs, it has been estimated that perhaps thousands of requests have arrived in your email, your postal mail, on the telephone, and maybe also at virtual small gatherings in the privacy of your own home where you do not even have to dress formally to attend the gala. Individuals who have long been deceased still receive calls or mail.

I am not blaming any organization who has not updated their massive lists, nor am I suggesting to decrease asking. If your job, if your heart, if your family, and if history exemplified giving, by all means, continue to give. The pandemic, unfortunately, will affect us for a very long time to come. The sadness of our losses will never completely leave us.

Giving of resources (time and money) will help us heal. Sharing in this way will bring us together whereas we have not been able to connect. Saying *thank you* may be two very small words that can travel the world and be remembered forever.

Try it. You will like it. It will make you feel very good.

8

When You Are Hungry

You do not have to be smart when you are hungry. You do not have to be a college student nor have multiple degrees. It might be helpful if you have street smarts or be clever. It might also help to be outgoing and willing to speak to strangers. I know these things not because I have been hungry for days on end, but I see a lot of hungry people simply by walking commercial streets or neighborhoods that house shops and restaurants in Los Angeles. These people are the new normal…the homeless—people with nowhere to live, nothing to eat, no resources to fall back on. They are on the corners, at the bus stops, and crowds of them, families, under freeway underpasses.

The Washington Post recently reported there are twenty-six million people experiencing lack of food in America. This recent term of food insecurity annoys me. It's not insecure about food. It's that you have no food. None. Frequently, they will stand in front of grocery stores or restaurants. It does not take much to figure out people exiting a grocery store may have spare change or items they are willing to give up. After all, how many boxes of cookies or loaves of bread do you really need or you can use fewer fresh carrots in the soup you plan to make. It takes little effort to give away duplicates to those "smart" enough to sit in the "good" locations. Just be aware. When you are hungry, you know these things. Now that this essay has reminded you of what has become a national characteristic and horribly exacerbated during the coronavirus, you, too, can think about them as you shop or pick up a birthday cake for someone you love. Maybe this essay will help you think a little differently.

Even before the coronavirus distancing rules, I think we were all aware of how many homeless were on the streets. During some counts, Los Angeles county reported 66,000 and growing. Many are older people. With the rise of unemployment and loss of wages with little warning and little savings existing, due to the coronavirus, even more are seen begging for money and food again and again. The same people on the same corners. I try to recall times I may have been hungry...when I have been overdrawn and also maxed out on credit cards. My financial acumen most of my life has been absent. Oh, I pretty much always had a job, a career even, but what I did not have was the ability to be smart about money. When I had it, I spent it; when I knew it was coming, I spent it. We did not go hungry.

When I was in fourth grade, our family had a tragedy, and we went from being upper middle class to having nothing—overnight with no warning. The next eight years were fraught with changing and accepting a totally different and traumatic reality. We had lost my father and our security. It took my mother a number of years to escape her shock and own the reality she was totally responsible for us. We always had a place to live in our own space. In the early years, we had family who helped us. During those years though, they became tired of supporting us in the myriad of ways necessary. They had their own needs and their own lives. I think over all they just became tired of us and our problems. By then my mother was front and center, responsible for our care and basically counted on no one but herself. "The hell with them all," she would say.

Unfortunately, I did not learn from her accomplishments. She always also said, "Don't we have enough to worry about?" So I became a good kid, never got in trouble, did not become wayward, nor stole or created acts of desperation. I felt lost, left out, alone, and different, not like regular kids who had a mother *and* a father. I did not compensate with trying harder, becoming smart, or applying myself rigorously. I functioned day by day, had to get a ride to Sunday School, knew there was no money for haircut or new clothes, and did not admit to being sick and taken to the doctor because seeing the doctor cost money and time away from my mother's job and thus her hourly salary. In high school, I could go for snacks with my friends, but I only had a coke while they had a burger and fries. I learned how best to compensate.

To this day, I am a survivor of this tragedy. My mentality is always in the survivor mode. I am accomplished and relatively secure but afraid to let myself believe I am financially okay, maybe even safe. I continue to believe all of us can end up on the street. One never knows what is coming down the track. Even if I think I am prepared for an emergency, I cannot ever forget that I, too, may end up on the street. It's a serious mental challenge to be secure and happy, even with a lot of therapy, but I more than manage and am not complaining. What I can easily admit to is *seeing* those who are hungry and acknowledging them. Some received a part of a birthday cake. Others I make sandwiches for and drop them at small tent sites. It does not take much, and it makes me feel better. And I hope they are less hungry at least for a while. You could do that too. Many people are helping, working at food banks, delivering masks, collecting nonperishable goods, and giving out bottles of water. I thank those hearty souls and hope you will too.

9

Does Sherri Smoke?

I am so depressed. I am smoking again. It has been a thirty-year battle to not smoke. I have tried all the well-known programs including hypnosis, smoke-enders, gum, mints, and the patch to stop. Unfortunately, I discovered I was allergic to the patch adhesive. My entire body itched so badly. I felt I needed to be hosed down. I had to get cortisone shots. No more patches. My grandma smoked until she died from heart issues. My father smoked then quit due to similar issues to his mom, but he always would sneak them but was not very clever about hiding the butts. He was always caught.

By now, if you are reading this, you know my age, so it's hard to give up a nasty habit after so many years. I think I started smoking when I was fourteen. Oh, it was quite cool back then. I adhered to most of the social etiquette rules for a female smoker. No smoking while walking down the street. Never smoking when wearing gloves, always smoking in restaurants, movie theaters, bars, after swimming, and, of course, after sex (not at fourteen). One more favorite place was in Las Vegas playing the slots and Blackjack, enjoying free alcohol, nervously deciding to take a hit on sixteen or not at all while smoking. I did not smoke during dread diseases. The stress of being sick sure made me want to. During two pregnancies, which were like a disease for me, I did not smoke. I was too sick, but occasionally I would flirt with the parking lot attendants at my workplace, and they would give me one. Again, I found a good alley and smoked half. Improvement, I thought. So that's the very short history of my smoking until March 2020 when COVID-19 hit, and we began the social isolation lockdown.

At first, it was not too difficult. I had paid my dues and was working, raising kids, and arranging birthday parties. And Let's not forget Halloween costumes, driving school car pools (do not call me Judge A. C. Barrett, please), and for soccer, baseball, tennis, Hebrew school, horseback riding, and street hockey. So having to stay at home, not even the pressure of a high-stress job, almost felt like a vacation or a sabbatical. I was okay. However, I did not really admit to knowing how bad it was and how much worse it was going to get. So naive. Really.

As of mid-March, my new normal was to sleep in, read books, watch movies, do a bit of writing, and promised myself no baking. Cooking, yes. Trying new recipes, yes but no baking of pastries, cookies, or cakes. Never the ever-popular challah baking; certainly, no sourdough. I do not even know what a starter is. If I had freshly baked, warm challah in the house, I would easily sit down with a tub of salted whipped butter and inhale that Jewish delicacy down. Six months into the lockdown, I delete all the virtual challah baking classes and proudly do not bake challah. I do, however, enjoy seeing my friend's creations on FB and am eternally grateful for those kind souls who offer me a home-baked challah.

By May, I was smoking a lot. *Okay*, maybe it was mid-April. I was very nervous about the rising numbers, increasing lockdowns, and frankly boring to tears with not enough to keep me busy nor out and about. When outside dining was suspended, I felt like a prisoner. Depressed, back to increased smoking—no longer adhering to three to five a day but eager for that first smoke as soon as I awakened. Never in the house but on the patio where our building is close to others, and I am surprised the neighbors have not thrown eggs at me. They do slam their open windows shut hard enough to crack the glass. So far no one has approached me to read me the riot act. My husband is amazingly silent: no bad looks, no coughing, and no lectures, and he has asthma. Jesus, what is wrong with me? My friends do not think I still smoke. I am a closet smoker.

My husband is not objective when it comes to me. This happens with third husbands who have never been married. They are so grateful to be married, not alone, and with a woman he adores. He actually totally accepts me—good and bad. He, too, has his faults. He whistles, and I wonder what the hell is he so happy about? As we shared the office, working remotely both of us, I would say to him, "Gee, honey, I did not know you whistled."

He would say, "I thought you liked it."

I would say, "Well, yes, when you were not home and out working. A little whistling was sweet, but now you are here all day and all night, this whistling is driving me crazy."

Did I mention I have very little work? I am a bit bored. I walk, almost daily, but even that has slowed down (it's pretty hot in Southern California). And the lack of walking may actually be showing as I try to wiggle into my jeans, even with no baking. You might be smoking too.

I have tons of groceries so I cook a lot. Some of us eat three meals a day, not I. So, a day or two of cooking and my husband has ample choice of what to eat *if* he could locate it in the refrigerator. I load and unload the dishwasher repeatedly. I take the trash out. My loving husband asks what he can do, but I say, "No, we are fine." He cannot cook beyond his morning eggs and oatmeal. I have demonstrated how to make tuna salad five times; he has written down the simple process, but it's clear, it's not going to happen. I have become Sherri housewife at your service! My angry tantrums are not something I am proud of at all. Pass the cigarettes, please.

Does anyone have any idea how expensive it is to smoke? It could be $11 for a pack, and of course, the cheaper ones give me a sore throat. Very few people know I smoke. I use a theory called "smokenspray." After a cigarette, I chew gum, the spicy kind that also makes my throat burn, then I spray my favorite lavender body spray. To this day, no one has said, "Jesus, you smell like a cigarette!" They may think it, but no one has said it. I smoke alone in my car but spray it afterward. One person did comment that my car smelled like perfume and cigarettes. Really?

Writing and not smoking is not easy. Our greatest authors smoked, drank whiskey, and wrote. Now who smokes anymore? The oddest thing has begun quite regularly with my increased COVID-19 smoking, never shared heretofore. When I smoke alone, out on my patio, I have amazing creative thoughts. Sometimes they feel almost magical. Such that often I come in and actually act upon them. I call someone I have been meaning to speak with. I have unusual and happy ideas for writing, or work projects/proposals, or who to reach out (talking/writing to strangers) even. It is uncanny. It's new and stronger as COVID-19 continues. Is this a new result of nicotine not yet discovered? Should I write to Dr. Fauci? On the morning smoke maybe, is it the combination of caffeine and nicotine? I even make deals with myself while smoking…write for one hour straight and then you can have lunch, be silent when wanting to make a critical comment to my husband for the day and then go get ice cream, and on and on. Care to join me? For the ice cream that is.

10

Only the Lonely

Dear friends and people I do not know who are alone,

I have spent parts of my life alone. Sometimes by choice and sometimes through circumstances. Sometimes, for example, during two of my marriages, I was alone even when I lived with my spouse. My spouses were very busy professionals and socially active in the community. I was home alone with the kids, having fun (oh, they were so cute, all three of them, and I love the memories) but feeling alone. It's not an uncommon problem. Sometimes I felt like the housekeeper even though we had a housekeeper for many years—always cleaning help. I do not clean. Straighten up and organize, *yes*. Clean, *no*.

So, in mid-March when we began social isolating as part of COVID-19, I did not feel like my life changed that much. I still worked at home alone, not such a big deal. I had worked remotely since 2010. I was used to it. I taught myself to have a routine and to have diversions—some inside the house where I had my remote office, other times outside, going to meetings with people, having lunch or other meals with people, going to exercise, or just speaking on the phone to friends. All these were important diversions. I listened to music often and took coffee breaks to read the paper. In my line of work, I needed to know what was happening in the world. This was all before COVID-19.

In a sense, COVID-19 ramped up my work. I called more people. I checked in on people I know who were elderly or alone. I cooked, froze, and kept chicken soup in my freezer to take to people recuperating from illness or as a check in. I always wore a mask and gloves. Being a remote worker, I liked being alone, but could build in breaks or work-related diversions to get me out of the house. Yes, there were days I wore pajamas. However, most days I was dressed with makeup and moving around which added tremendously to my productivity. My work life was pretty flexible. No one was calling me, asking what I had accomplished. Supervision was pretty casual. Every month, I completed the dreaded KPI (key performance index). I never knew if anyone even read it. Over one four-year period, no one ever complained. Truth be told, I liked working alone. My husband was a nine-to-five worker. He was gone all day, home in the evening.

When I was young and growing up, everyone in my small family seemed to have somewhere to be or to go, and I was by myself often. Both my parents worked in their high-stress business of mom-and-pop grocery stores. My sister was charming and beautiful and had a full social life and was never around unless my parents made her stay home to watch me. Such enforced togetherness was never pleasant. We both felt we were serving a sentence similar to prison. When I was in the fourth grade, my father left us. He was gone for eight years while he explored the world and his life as though he were a man with no responsibilities. He never sent money let alone a birthday card. Pretty traumatic for a young girl who was in love with her daddy and dreamed about marrying him.

And so, in March of this year, when the world began to social distance, I was experienced at being alone. My contract work all dried up, but I had many activities, friends to speak to, and did not worry about being alone. I became active in an active older adult group. I loved to read, and in some ways, it's a solitary activity. In other ways, it's a fantasy life, reading the lives and experiences of others. But because as I approached my seventy-fifth birthday, I was reminded of how I never expected to live a long life. Over time, I had a number of serious illnesses. Well, I thought a pandemic is a perfect way to die. So many are doing it. It's almost a popular alternative for those of us who consider dying quite regularly. It's the final goodbye and why not have it occur when it would not be my fault. I did not want to be accused of "had I done a better job of taking care of myself," I would not have died. It would be a blameless death, almost popular. The masses are dying, sort of it's happening to everyone. Crazy thoughts, right? But better than being alone? We are approaching 2021, and I am still here. And many are still alone. Some are even embarrassed to ask for help.

I have a better, more stable life than perhaps ever before. I do not walk around the house in the middle of the night studying the checkbook. I am married for the third time and quite content. Perhaps for the first time ever, the glass is not half empty. My husband will not be leaving me like the others. He is too settled and too polite even to consider the tragedy of divorce, and his love is honorable and genuine. We have a full life together. We can be alone together even, and I do not feel I am by myself. However, my husband retired, and now he was home as well. Suddenly, I was no longer home alone. We shared the office space. He was here all the time. Being extra safe, he rarely went out. We took a few walks, but he is a much faster walker than I. We shared Zoom calls of concerts, travel opportunities, and many speakers on political issues.

Then the pandemic and suddenly the world was working at home. Some with no preparation even for how you structure your day without coworkers and a lunch break. Then you cease working and go home, picking up another life of other responsibilities, entertainment, and social activities. Many were working with little supervision, experiencing freedom for the first time while working. They had no idea what to do with it. They could take a break and run an errand. However, in social isolation, there are few places to go—everything is shut down. You could pick up takeout from a favorite restaurant and go for a walk. That's it. But don't forget your mask and gloves.

Some businesses and certainly those more formal quickly instituted policy for how to work at home. This was considered the opposite end of the spectrum. You had to fill out an online form to advise a manager (also working at home) if you were off the grid for fifteen-minute (or more) increments. At the end of the day, you were required to send in three major areas you accomplished and at least two areas of carryover for the next day. Was there anyone on the other end? Were they reading this? You had to send a list of attempted phone calls. You had to send a list of connected phone calls and the results. You did not have to let them know the number of bathroom breaks nor how often you washed your hands.

And then there are the older adults—many living alone, relatives far away. They say isolation can be worse for your health than smoking ten cigarettes a day.

Can you imagine? In California, it is estimated 1.2 million older people live alone. Creative nonprofits and places of worship quickly assembled buddy and check in calls. Callers receive training and or talking points. Today in our crazy world, you cannot be so sure who is contacting you. Elder abuse is more than frequent. One older woman on my call list asked me, "What exactly do you want me to do?" I gently explained I was calling to offer her any help she might need like groceries or even picking up the dry cleaning. That is what I could do for her. Callers must be gentle and focused and mainly expressing support. That can be a challenge when you are speaking to a stranger.

I have had lower back issues. I go to physical therapy twice a week. I shower on those days. I get out and see people on the street—other drivers in the new Los Angeles normal of little traffic. I discover new restaurants open for takeout. My physical therapist has become my new go-to Dear Abby. I tell her home alone stories. I show her photos and videos of my seventeen-month-old granddaughter living three thousand miles away with her parents, my children. Sometimes I even bring cookies. She is a wonderful listener and shares a bit of her own life as she stretches my muscles.

Overall, I am comfortable. I can be alone—not jumping out of my skin nor turning into a cranky older adult. I am older, and I do get cranky (when will the mail be delivered). I hope our social isolation will be over soon, when it is safe. It will not be going back to the same-old, same-old. There will be a new normal even though I am not certain what it will be. I do hope and maybe even pray fewer people are sick and die or have to die alone. I am content and grateful to still be here. Maybe even see my granddaughter in person, up close with lots of kisses, touching our faces. I hope that will be the case for many.

See you soon (I hope) in person,
Sherri

11

Needles

Needles really scare me. I have had too many. My brother-in-law, a doctor, told me I was like a cat who had nine lives. He also said pregnancy (twice) was a disease for me. I was a high-risk, older mom, developing a wide array of issues not really related to the fetus but exacerbated by being pregnant. I had severe endometriosis as a teenager and surgery for that. I contracted pneumonia more than once. I had cysts on my kidney and surgery for that. I had cancer and most recently severe back issues. And a spine specialist injected me eight times across my lower back to reduce the pain. Those are but a few of my needle stories. They bring back bad memories. Enough, right?

Now with the help of God and modern science, I will of course receive the vaccine when I can. But yes, I will be scared and flooded with anxiety. This is a needle, which may just prevent COVID-19 and not dying what appears to be a horrible death. I want that needle. The virus death will not be like a movie with a beautiful woman lying on clean white sheets, lovely hair, nicely arranged, fanned out on the pillow, waiting for the final moment. We have seen the photographs of very sick people many about to die with tubes, masks, and ventilators. The needle will sting. It will feel very cold going in. It will make me recall painful thoughts of other more seriously and dreaded needles.

Did you know when you undergo surgery for breast cancer, before you are put to sleep, a nurse must map the tumor as prep for the surgeon? It helps him quickly identify where to cut. Let me repeat, you are awake and on high alert, very aware of the procedure. I screamed and cried as a very insensitive nurse repeatedly stuck needles into my breast.

So, when I think of the vaccine, these heinous needle nightmares invariably return. I will do it, take the vaccine of course, but knowing me, doing whatever necessary to decrease my memories, I might have a little wine or even take medication to relax me. It will be better than the fear and anxiety. Bring it on! I am ready!

12

Forgiveness

Will I forgive all those denying the virus and not wearing masks? What did I learn during the pandemic? Sometimes I was extremely patient and sensitive. As time moved forward, I was not so motivated, and cranky (to use a polite word) was creeping in during many conversations and silly arguments about how best to make tuna salad. Did I use all this free unstructured time well? Clean out files, cabinets, or attempt the great American novel? Did I miss the holidays? Yes. Did I call friends and not-so-close friends? Yes. Were they grateful? You betcha!

Will COVID-19 cause us to forgive? Given our fears and insecurities during this plague, will it cause us to be more forgiving? Will I and many others who experience the plague cause us to be kinder, more giving? More generous in thought and spirit? More grateful for what we have? More active in encouraging volunteerism: writing thousands of postcards urging people to vote, delivering groceries to shut-ins, serving meals at food sites, tutoring children who have no access to online devices, and much more. Many institutions and organizations jumped in immediately to teach older people to use the computer so they would have a means to see friends, listen to fun speakers, culture and art, and candid concrete safety information. These agencies became saviors. Perhaps, this is the silver lining.

Will we forgive POTUS for thinking the virus will just disappear when the weather is warmer? Will we forgive him for not advocating wearing masks? Will we forgive our congressional representatives for sitting on their hands, not immediately providing allocations to alleviate the suffering of no jobs, no food, nor housing? No forgiveness on this end. I do not forgive the orthopedist for referring to my back injury as unremarkable. I never forgave my father for abandoning us. When he returned to make amends and reunite with my mother, I accepted him. But never forgave him for altering my life, creating characteristics that affect me, staying with me to this day.

Why was our country, the most modern, the most powerful, supposedly the richest, and the most technologically advanced, yet not have enough supplies or be prepared for a disaster that would take thousands of loved ones from our lives? I do not forgive our country for lack of preparedness. How can we not fear for the well-being of the doctors, nurses, healthcare professionals, and even those who merely transferred the sick and dying?—our frontline caregivers! What commitment and dedication these proud people must have! They are role models for us all.

13

Morr Musings

These little incidents and daydreaming could all be sent to those who write advice columns. These sightings are both humorous and annoying, causing one to nod their heads and agree...yes, that happens in our house too. Trapped with coworkers and family, including one's children (small or large), appears to have no good answers.

❧ My coworker whistles. It's very annoying. Sometimes he also jiggles his foot against the steel desk, making noises that distract me from my own work. He often asks what's for lunch. When he unloads the dishwasher, the counters look like Bed Bath & Beyond. With no coupon. I still love him. After all he is my husband.

❧ Why are cruise ships still advertising discounts and deals?

❧ In the last six years or so, I began to chew ice. It has become a nervous habit. It's like swishing your hair from side to side but much louder. I rationalize it as exercise for your teeth. My teeth are far from great, but I swear, it is making my teeth stronger. However, I am chilled afterward.

ᎧᏖ Why are periodicals and newsletters asking for donations when so many people need jobs, food, or housing?

ᎧᏖ The span of insurance offers clearly is not missing any opportunities. Can we apply for life insurance during the pandemic?

ᎧᏖ Shopping, shopping, and more shopping. Where do these advertisers think we are going that we would need fancy dresses, socks, and shoes? Coats, boots, and heavy winter gear in Los Angeles? What I really need is a new beach chair to be at the ready when the beaches are again open.

ᎧᏖ When it's summer, my coworker lifts weights on our small patio. He has stolen my space for sneaking cigarettes.

ᎧᏖ Why does my hair look so good on Zoom calls?

ᎧᏖ Some years ago, a millennial commented that she loved my unusual array of necklaces. "Honey," I said, "when you have had as many husbands as I have, you, too, will have such a collection." Of necklaces, that is. *Yikes*. Did I really say that?

❧ Fat chunks of avocado on icy-cold gazpacho soup have been my newest invention. After all, since I declared, "There will be no baking in this house," I have to make something for us to eat.

❧ Next to my young adult children and my grandchildren, I miss movies the most. Sitting in a dark space, comfy cushy chairs, most with cup holders, and popcorn, alone even or with friends, there is nothing better. In a two-hour span, you can experience love, romance, violence, killings (sometimes even deserved), drugs, blood, humor, singing and dancing, amazing score, and yes *sex*, all in two hours. It's worth whatever it takes (and costs) to get there. Hand-holding is also good.

❧ My coworker is always cold; therefore, even in "wintery" California, he wants the heat at seventy-five, day and night. Such high temperatures cause my nose to totally dry out, causing little flakes like dandruff to drip out. At times, all I want to do is blow my nose. He sleeps in very warm pajamas and a hoodie and has extra blankets, and still I am sneaking the heat down as often as possible.

❧ One day out walking in broad daylight, a strange man pulled to the curb where I was walking, rolled down his window, and asked, "Do you need a ride?" I smirked, said no, and kept walking. I continued walking maybe a quicker pace, then I freaked out, checked to see if he was following me, and advanced my pace. I now carry one of those screeching alarms hooked to my jeans.

ॐ My coworker is great at fixing many things. When the slats fall off the window shades, no one fixes them better.

ॐ In February, I declared we must take a break from having guests for dinner. So much work: the menus, the shopping, the cooking, and the cleanup. They're all great friends, and it's a lot of fun. It takes me three days to get it done the way I like it. Plus accommodating vegans, dairy-free, no red meat, gluten-free (which costs a hell of a lot more), no white sugar, no citrus, and no garlic. Now about to enter 2021, oh, how I would love to have those people in my house, joyously eating what they can.

ॐ I found it very annoying that when POTUS was ill with COVID-19 and in the hospital after testing positive, we heard so little about Melania who also tested positive. We knew she was quarantined, but did she have a fever, a sore throat, any symptoms? Who was taking care of her? Later there was a puffy piece in *Vanity Fair* magazine, and FOX said a few things, or was it CNN? Had it been Hilary or Michelle or even Laura? Believe me, we would have been storming the White House to make sure she is okay! She is the FLOTUS for god's sake.

ॐ I have three gifts: Jay, Jesse, and Noah. Each in their own right a treasure. Three active boys, young men now who taught me what love truly is. One was adopted when few newborns were available. The other two were both high-risk pregnancies resulting in early delivery. Today they are thriving in their personal and professional lives. In my "seventy-five and fabulous" years, there is no more exemplary accomplishment.

᪥ A man is sleeping in his car outside our house. I can see him from our window. I want to go out and give him a pillow and a blanket. But I am afraid.

᪥ In Israel, the Hebrew word *matzav* means the situation. Instead of being specific and instead of saying I am opposed to the occupation, or it is so expensive to live here, or the worst the constant fear of terror and war, one knows that the *matzav* covers and is interpreted as all of these daily issues. Over the last year, I have felt I had my own *matzav*. My situation, like millions of others, was fear of getting the virus, COVID-19. My charisma, my style, is to be a see-and-be-seen person. I am generally out and about a lot. In a nanosecond, that was to be no more. Then I had a series of medical issues where I did go out but to doctors two or three times a week. In February of 2020, I had a slight fall. It took a whole year to recover. With all that, I had some very down days, but I always reminded myself how lucky I was to be alive and not bundled in tubes and intubation, waiting to die from the virus. Now I am vaccinated and less down, more hopeful, grateful to be loved by my coworker, happy to have shelter and food, and not fearful of ending up on the street. So my situation is not so bad at all.

About the Author

Sherri Morr has been a writer since she was in her late twenties. In *75 and Fabulous: Reflections*, it is the first time her work has left the computer and was published.

During her career as a professional fundraiser, she wrote many essays and training manuals about being a successful fundraiser. Morr shared humorous stories about managing donors who gave large sums of money to nonprofits and expected special treatment and acceptance. She wrote and published a series of articles about remote working prior to the pandemic when workers worldwide were made to leave their offices safe and socially isolated.

Her unique voice shared personal and painful expectations during a family tragedy that affected her growing-up years. These years mirrored thousands of seasonal and low-income workers who lost their money in a nanosecond with no warning and little if any savings at the pandemic's start. Her desire to read memoirs, life stories of women's struggles, has given her the courage to write with truth and fear, given the success of many women who overcame tragic loss and disruption.

Morr had written a story about forgiveness, which has become a standard of the salon theater for The Braid in Santa Monica, California, performed annually over eight years. She presented a humorous story, "Canned Fruit," for a three-hundred-person audience at National Public Radio Moth Theater in Washington, DC.